Passport to Purpose

Leadership, Faith, and the Journey of Becoming

By Clémentine Uwineza

Dedication

To the One who never left my side—
my Creator, my Redeemer, my constant Companion.
You carried me from refugee camps to boardrooms,
from whispered prayers to entrusted responsibility.
This passport is stamped with grace.

And to those who rebuild when the cost is high,
who carry responsibility before recognition,
who lead with faith even when the way is unclear—
this journey is for you.

You are not unseen.
You belong.
You are being led.

Vision to Execution Collection

This book is part of the **Vision to Execution Collection** – a body of work centered on faith, leadership, and the intentional design of a life aligned with purpose, excellence, and sustainability.

Each book represents a distinct stage in a transformational journey:

Lifted to Lift Others

The Foundation – Encounter and Transformation

A powerful testimony of resilience, faith, and God's transforming grace. This book reveals how purpose is often born through adversity, and how what we overcome becomes part of what we are called to give.

→ *Where purpose begins through healing, restoration, and encounter with God.*

Passport to Purpose

The Journey – Identity and Leadership Formation

A leadership-centered exploration of how life experiences shape identity, calling, and influence.

Through transitions, challenges, and growth, this book helps readers recognize that their journey is not random – it is preparation.

→ *Where purpose is understood, embraced, and developed into leadership.*

The Quality of a Life
The System — Stewardship and Sustainable Living

A practical framework for designing a life that sustains purpose over time. Drawing from both life experience and disciplined systems thinking, this book equips readers to build habits, structures, and standards that prevent burnout and enable lasting impact.

> → *Where purpose is lived daily with clarity, discipline, and excellence.*

A Complete Journey

Together, these books form a unified path:

Encounter → Identity → Stewardship

A journey from being transformed,
to understanding purpose,
to living it intentionally every day.

TABLE OF CONTENTS

A Note to the Reader: How to Read This Book

This book is written as a journey, not a formula.

Passport to Purpose does not offer a step-by-step guide to success, nor does it present leadership as a destination to be reached. Instead, it traces how purpose is carried—across borders, seasons, responsibilities, and identities—and how leadership is shaped through faithfulness over time.

You will encounter story, reflection, and practice woven together. The narrative chapters follow my lived journey—from formation and survival, through rebuilding and professional growth, into leadership shaped by integrity and global responsibility. Along the way, you will find recurring elements that invite you to pause and reflect on your own path.

Each chapter includes:

A Leadership Lesson – *not a theory, but a truth drawn from lived experience*

Visas and Stamps – *symbolic permissions and affirmations meant to name growth and identity*

Practices and Rituals – *moments to slow down and apply what resonates*

Prayers and Reflections – *offered as grounding, not instruction*

These elements are optional but intentional. You may read this book straight through, or you may return to specific chapters as your own journey unfolds. There is no required pace.

This is also not a book that rushes resolution. Some chapters sit with uncertainty, cost, and responsibility without immediately resolving them. That is deliberate. Purpose is rarely revealed all at once. It is clarified through endurance, humility, and service.

You do not need to share my background, profession, or faith tradition to find meaning here. What matters is the willingness to reflect honestly on where you are, what you carry, and how you lead—whether visibly or quietly.

If you are navigating transition, carrying responsibility, questioning belonging, or leading without a clear map, this book is meant to walk with you, not ahead of you.

Read with patience.
Pause when something resonates.
Carry forward what is yours to keep.

The journey will continue long after the final page.

Chapter 1: The House with Seven Children

Leadership Lesson: Leadership is often formed long before it is named, through responsibility, discipline, and example.

Where My Leadership Story Began

I was born in Rwanda, a country rich in culture, resilience, and community. My earliest memories are rooted in a lively household filled with responsibility, faith, and shared life. I grew up in a home with seven children, where everyone had a role to play and a contribution to make. Our house was rarely quiet and rarely empty. Family members, neighbors, and friends came and went freely, and hospitality was a natural part of everyday life rather than a special occasion.

My parents created an environment where values were lived rather than explained. My father, a mechanical engineer and director at a dealership center, modeled integrity through consistency and discipline. My mother, a manager at the city postal office, led with structure, firmness, and care. They provided stability for our family, but more importantly, they established a foundation of character, service, and faith that shaped who we became.

At the time, I did not think of this environment as leadership training. Looking back, I now understand that this was where my leadership journey truly began.

Discipline as a Way of Life

Discipline in our household was not punitive or harsh. It was simply how life was organized. Every child had responsibilities, and participation was expected from everyone. Chores were part of daily routine, and accountability was non-negotiable. We learned early that contribution mattered and that shared responsibility strengthened the household.

I spent many hours helping with cleaning, cooking, and caring for younger children. These tasks taught me humility, consistency, and respect for work that often goes unseen. My parents did not frame discipline as punishment, but as preparation. Through repetition and structure, they instilled habits that later became essential in my personal and professional life.

My mother corrected with clarity and firmness, while offering encouragement quietly. My father spoke little but demonstrated his values through his actions. From them, I learned that leadership does not require constant instruction; it requires integrity that can be observed and trusted.

Faith as the Foundation

Faith was central to our family life. Attending church on Sundays was expected, but faith extended well beyond weekly services. It influenced how we treated others, how we resolved conflict, and how we understood responsibility and accountability.

Church was a place where I learned patience, discipline, and respect for authority. I learned how to listen, how to observe, and how to use my voice thoughtfully. Faith also gave us a shared sense of belonging and purpose that connected our family to a larger community.

More importantly, faith gave us an anchor. It taught us that life had meaning beyond circumstance and that character mattered even when no one was watching. Those lessons would later become essential when life demanded resilience beyond anything I could have anticipated.

The First Leadership Classroom

The first place I learned leadership was not a school or workplace. It was our home. Leadership was practiced through daily actions rather than formal instruction. I learned leadership by sharing resources, completing responsibilities without complaint, and caring for others when it was inconvenient.

These early experiences taught me that leadership is not defined by authority or recognition. It is defined by responsibility, trust, and service. Before I ever led teams or projects, I learned how to contribute to something larger than myself.

The values formed in that household shaped the way I would later show up in academic environments, professional settings, and leadership roles. Discipline became a habit. Service became instinctive. Faith became the foundation for decision-making.

What I Did Not Understand at the Time

As a child, I did not realize how much these early years were preparing me for the future. I did not know that everything familiar would one day be disrupted. I did not know that safety would be replaced by uncertainty or that survival would require courage beyond routine.

What I did know was that I was loved, supported, and grounded. Those roots would matter far more than circumstances when everything else was stripped away.

Looking back, I can see that this season laid the groundwork for what was to come. The stability of my early life built internal resilience. The discipline and faith that shaped me in ordinary times would later sustain me through extraordinary challenges.

●●●

🛂 VISA OF ROOTS — Permission to Honor Your Beginning

Visa Granted:
I give myself permission to honor the people, places, and values that shaped my early life. My beginnings were not insignificant; they were formative and meaningful.

🕊 STAMP OF FORMATION

Stamp: Leadership begins in the ordinary.

> ***Scripture:***
> *"Whoever can be trusted with very little can also be trusted with much." — Luke 16:10*

✨ RITUAL — The Memory Mapping Practice

Set aside time this week to reflect on an early experience that influenced your character or sense of responsibility. Consider what you learned in that moment and how it continues to shape the way you lead, work, or relate to others today.

🙏 PRAYER OF GRATITUDE FOR ORIGINS

> *God, thank You for the people and environments that shaped my early years. Thank You for the discipline, faith, and values that formed my character long before I understood their importance. Help me honor my beginnings and carry forward what was planted in me*

with humility and purpose. May my life reflect the foundation that was laid in those early seasons. Amen.

📓 REFLECTION CHECKPOINT

What early responsibilities shaped your character?

Which values were modeled for you before they were explained?

How did your upbringing prepare you for leadership, even before you recognized it?

What part of your origin story deserves renewed appreciation?

🌟 LIFTED LESSON

Wisdom: Leadership is developed through consistency and responsibility long before it is publicly recognized.

In Practice: Pay attention to how you handle everyday responsibilities; these moments continue to shape your leadership.

Action: Identify one value from your upbringing and intentionally apply it this week.

Scripture:
"Train up a child in the way he should go..." – Proverbs 22:6

Chapter 2: When the World Shook

Leadership Lesson: Crisis does not create character; it reveals it. Compassion, steadiness, and moral clarity define leadership when fear dominates.

The Day Everything Changed

There are moments in life that permanently divide time into "before" and "after." For me, that moment came when I was a teenager in Rwanda and the world I knew collapsed.

The 1994 **Rwandan genocide** (also known as the **Tutsi genocide**) was not a spontaneous outbreak of violence. Genocide is the intentional, systematic attempt to destroy an entire group of people based on ethnicity, identity, or belief. In Rwanda, it unfolded with devastating speed and precision. In a matter of weeks, more than a million lives were lost. Communities were dismantled. Families were destroyed. Neighbors turned against neighbors.

One day, I was a student with routines, expectations, and dreams. The next, the very fabric of society had unraveled. Streets that once felt familiar became dangerous. Silence replaced laughter. Fear replaced certainty.

At that age, I understood enough to know that what was happening was not ordinary conflict. It was deliberate. It was organized. And it was terrifying.

From Genocide to War: The Flight to Congo

When the genocide ended, the violence did not immediately stop. What followed was war. Armed conflict spread across the region, and instability intensified. It was during this period—after the genocide, as war erupted—that my family fled Rwanda.

We ran for our lives into the forests of Congo. We did not leave because it was safe elsewhere. We left because staying meant risking death. We carried almost nothing with us. Our home, our belongings, and our sense of security were left behind.

What we carried instead was fear, faith, and each other.

Survival became our only objective.

Life in the Refugee Camps

The refugee camps in Congo were nothing like the life I had known. Hunger was constant. Disease spread quickly. Privacy disappeared. Thousands of people lived side by side, united by loss and uncertainty.

I witnessed children die from starvation and illness. I saw parents make impossible decisions. I saw desperation strip people of dignity. But even in that environment, something remarkable persisted.

People shared food they barely had. Mothers cared for children who were not their own. Strangers offered protection when no formal system existed. In the darkness, prayers were whispered quietly, often without words.

Humanity was deeply wounded—but it was not extinguished.

In those camps, I learned that leadership does not require authority. It requires presence. It requires compassion. It requires the willingness to care for others even when you yourself are afraid.

Learning to Lead Without Power

There were no formal leaders in the camps who could guarantee safety or stability. Leadership emerged organically through calmness and selflessness. Those who could remain steady in chaos became anchors for others.

I watched adults share what little they had and children help younger ones survive. I learned that leadership in crisis is not about giving orders. It is about remaining grounded when fear overwhelms.

One night remains especially clear in my memory. We were huddled together, exhausted and hungry. Fear pressed in from every side.

My mother reached for my hand and whispered that God was still with us.

I did not understand how she could believe that. But I held her hand tightly.

That moment taught me a truth I would carry for the rest of my life: leadership often begins not with solutions, but with reassurance.

Faith as a Conscious Choice

During that season, faith was not emotional or expressive. It was intentional. It was choosing to believe that God was present even when evidence suggested otherwise. It was choosing hope when despair felt more reasonable.

Fear did not disappear. Hunger did not disappear. Danger did not disappear. But faith allowed us to move forward without being consumed by them.

Years later, I would find words that described what we lived through: "I know what it is to be in need, and I know what it is to have plenty... I can do all this through Him who gives me strength." At the time, I did not have that language. But I lived its truth.

Faith was not a feeling. It was a decision.

Returning to a Changed Home

Eventually, we returned to Rwanda. The country we came back to was profoundly changed. Our home in the capital had been destroyed. We settled in a new town and began again with very little.

Survival left scars. I was no longer the same girl who had left. I had seen loss, cruelty, and fragility up close. Yet I was not consumed by bitterness. I was deeply grateful.

I had learned that safety is never guaranteed. I had learned that contentment is not tied to possessions. And I had learned that faith is not about comfort—it is about trust.

That season refined me. It revealed strengths I did not know I possessed and values that would later define my leadership.

What Crisis Revealed About Leadership

Crisis revealed that leadership is not about certainty or control. It is about compassion, steadiness, and responsibility in moments of fear. People may forget words, but they remember presence.

The lessons from that time continue to shape how I lead today. In professional environments, I remain calm under pressure, attentive to people, and focused on empathy. What was formed in survival later became service.

I did not know it then, but this season was preparing me for what came next. What was forged in fear would later become empathy. What was learned in crisis would later guide leadership.

Survival had kept us alive. Rebuilding would require something different.

●●●

🛂 VISA OF RESILIENCE — Permission to Rise from Ruins

Visa Granted:
I give myself permission to acknowledge my pain without allowing it to define me. I am allowed to rebuild, to hope again, and to carry forward the strength born from adversity.

🕊 STAMP OF COURAGE

Stamp: Compassion leads even in crisis.

> ***Scripture:***
> *"The light shines in the darkness, and the darkness has not overcome it." – John 1:5*

✨ RITUAL — The Courage-in-Crisis Reflection

When facing uncertainty or fear, reflect on the following:

> *Who around me needs calm presence right now?*
>
> *What small act of compassion can I offer?*
>
> *What truth can anchor me when circumstances feel unstable?*

🙏 PRAYER FOR STRENGTH IN DIFFICULT SEASONS

> *God, when the world feels unstable, steady my heart. When fear rises, remind me that You are present. Teach me to lead with compassion even when I am hurting. Help me trust You through rebuilding and give me the courage to move forward, one step at a time. Amen.*

📓 REFLECTION CHECKPOINT

> *What crisis revealed something important about my character?*
>
> *How did compassion show up for me during hardship?*
>
> *What strengths were formed in me through adversity?*
>
> *How can I use my experiences to lead others with empathy?*

🌟 LIFTED LESSON

Wisdom: Crisis reveals true leadership and refines character.

In Practice: In moments of pressure, prioritize empathy and presence over control.

Action: Offer support to someone facing difficulty this week.

> **Scripture:**
> *"The Lord is close to the brokenhearted."* — Psalm 34:18

Chapter 3: The Return and the Call

Leadership Lesson: Adaptability is a foundational leadership skill. The ability to rebuild, learn, and respond faithfully to change determines long-term impact.

Coming Home to a New Reality

When we returned to Rwanda after the genocide and the subsequent war, we did not return to the life we had left behind. The country was still healing. Communities were fractured. Loss was visible in both physical structures and human expressions.

Our home in the capital had been destroyed. What once represented safety and stability no longer existed. We settled instead in a rural area, starting again with very little. Familiar routines were replaced by uncertainty, and rebuilding became part of daily life.

Although we were home geographically, nothing felt the same. Survival had altered our perspective. We carried memories that could not be undone, and we faced a future that felt fragile and undefined. Yet, we were alive. And that mattered.

Learning to Live With Less—and With Meaning

Returning to school became a critical part of my healing and rebuilding. Education offered structure in a world that had lost predictability. Each day in the classroom was an act of defiance against despair and an affirmation that the future was still worth investing in.

I studied with intensity and purpose. Not because I knew exactly where education would take me, but because learning restored a sense of agency. It reminded me that my life was still unfolding.

Living with less stripped life down to what mattered most. I learned to appreciate small victories, simple routines, and moments of peace. I learned that joy does not require abundance and that progress does not always happen quickly.

This season taught me contentment, not as resignation, but as strength.

The Quiet Emergence of a Calling

During this time, I began to sense that my life was moving in a new direction, even though I could not yet name it. I no longer dreamed only of personal success. Survival had expanded my perspective. I felt a growing responsibility to live in a way that honored the fact that I had survived.

I did not experience a dramatic calling or a defining spiritual moment. Instead, purpose emerged quietly. It appeared in my renewed commitment to education, in my growing curiosity about the world beyond Rwanda, and in my willingness to say yes to opportunities I had never imagined for myself. I began to understand that calling is often revealed through obedience rather than certainty.

Saying Yes to the Unknown

The opportunity to go to the United States came unexpectedly. It was not something I had actively pursued, nor something I felt fully prepared for. I had imagined Europe—countries where language and culture felt more familiar. America felt distant, foreign, and intimidating.

English was not my language. The culture was unfamiliar. The distance from home felt overwhelming.

Yet, the opportunity was undeniable.

I felt both excitement and fear. I knew that accepting meant leaving what little familiarity I had rebuilt. It meant stepping into uncertainty once again. But I had learned something important through loss and survival: fear does not always mean stop. Sometimes, it means prepare.

I said yes—not because I felt confident, but because I trusted that the same God who had carried me through crisis would not abandon me in transition.

Becoming Someone New

Agreeing to leave Rwanda marked the beginning of a transformation that extended far beyond geography. It required me to release the version of myself that clung to familiarity and to embrace growth without guarantees.

I was no longer just a survivor returning home. I was becoming a student of the world. A learner. A woman being shaped for something larger than she could yet understand.

That decision—to say yes without clarity—would become a pattern in my life. It would later influence how I approached leadership, career changes, and global opportunities. Adaptability became not just a skill, but a way of living.

I did not know it then, but this moment was preparing me for the next stage of my journey. What began as rebuilding would soon require courage. What was restored in quiet places would soon be tested in unfamiliar ones.

VISA OF TRANSFORMATION — Permission to Grow Beyond What Is Familiar

Visa Granted:
I give myself permission to grow beyond the limits of my past and the boundaries of comfort.

I am allowed to evolve, adapt, and become more than I once imagined.

🕊️STAMP OF COURAGEOUS OBEDIENCE

Stamp: Growth often begins with a faithful yes.

> **Scripture:**
> *"Have I not commanded you? Be strong and courageous. Do not be afraid... for the Lord your God will be with you wherever you go." – Joshua 1:9*

✨ RITUAL – The "Yes" Reflection

When facing an unfamiliar opportunity, pause and consider:

> *Is this an open door, even if it feels uncomfortable?*
>
> *Am I hesitating because of fear or lack of trust?*
>
> *What might growth require of me in this season?*

Write down one area of your life where you are being invited to say yes despite uncertainty.

🙏 PRAYER FOR COURAGE AND TRUST

> *God, thank You for guiding me through seasons of rebuilding and transition. When the path ahead is unclear, help me trust You rather than my comfort. Give me the courage to say yes when You open doors and the humility to grow into the person You are shaping me to be. Let my obedience lead me forward. Amen.*

📓 REFLECTION CHECKPOINT

What season of rebuilding has shaped my resilience?

Where have I been invited to grow beyond what feels familiar?

What fears have held me back from saying yes?

How might adaptability strengthen my leadership today?

✨ LIFTED LESSON

Wisdom: Adaptability is not weakness; it is leadership in motion.

In Practice: Growth often requires releasing certainty before clarity arrives.

Action: Identify one area where you are resisting change and take one intentional step forward this week.

Scripture:
"*See, I am doing a new thing.*" – Isaiah 43:19

Chapter 4: Boarding the Unknown

Leadership Lesson: Leadership often begins before clarity arrives. Courage is not the absence of fear, but the willingness to move forward despite it.

Leaving What Was Familiar

Leaving Rwanda for the United States was not simply a change of location. It was a departure from everything familiar—language, culture, relationships, and identity. Although I had already experienced displacement, this transition felt different. This time, I was leaving by choice, not by force. That distinction carried both privilege and responsibility.

I had never been on an airplane before. The idea of flying across the world felt abstract and overwhelming. I did not fully understand what awaited me, only that my life was about to change again. I carried a single suitcase, limited English, and a quiet determination shaped by everything I had already survived.

As I prepared to leave, I felt the weight of what I was stepping into. I was not only representing myself. I was carrying the hopes of my family and the expectations that come with being given an opportunity that many never receive.

The Journey Across Borders

The journey itself became a lesson in humility and adaptability. Traveling through international airports exposed how dependent I was on others. I could not read signs easily. I could not ask questions with confidence. I relied on gestures, patience, and the kindness of strangers.

Each layover reminded me how small I felt in a vast world. Yet, each successful connection reinforced something important: I was capable of learning, adjusting, and continuing forward even when I felt out of place.

By the time we landed in the United States, exhaustion mixed with awe. Everything felt larger, faster, and unfamiliar. The scale of the highways, the cold air, and the quiet efficiency of daily life contrasted sharply with what I had known.

I realized quickly that arrival did not mean understanding. It simply meant the journey had entered a new phase.

Entering a New World

My first days in America were filled with observation. I watched how people spoke, how they interacted, how systems functioned. I noticed how direct communication was valued and how independence was expected. Everything required adjustment, from food to schedules to social norms.

Language was the most immediate barrier. I could understand very little and express even less. Each interaction required focus and courage. Simple tasks demanded energy. Mistakes were frequent and humbling.

Yet, beneath the discomfort, something steady remained. I had learned through previous upheaval that unfamiliarity does not equal impossibility. Survival had taught me resilience. Rebuilding had taught me patience. Now, adaptation would teach me growth.

Faith as a Constant in Transition

Although everything around me was changing, my faith remained constant. It did not remove uncertainty, but it provided orientation. When I did not know what to expect, faith reminded me that I was not navigating alone.

I prayed often, not with elaborate words, but with simple honesty. I asked for understanding, endurance, and clarity. Faith did not immediately answer every question, but it anchored me when answers were slow to arrive.

This season reinforced a truth I would carry into leadership roles later in life: confidence does not require full understanding. It requires trust and consistency.

Beginning Without Certainty

Starting life in a new country required accepting that I would not feel competent right away. I had to become comfortable being a beginner again. That meant asking questions, making mistakes, and resisting the urge to retreat when things felt difficult.

I learned that leadership growth often begins with humility. Before leading others, you must be willing to learn. Before influencing systems, you must be willing to navigate them as an outsider.

I did not know what my education or career would look like yet. I only knew that growth required movement, and movement required courage.

Looking back, I see clearly that this moment was not about arrival—it was about readiness. What I learned in this transition would later shape how I approached unfamiliar environments, global work, and leadership under uncertainty.

VISA OF COURAGE — Permission to Begin Without Clarity

Visa Granted:
I give myself permission to move forward even when I do not have all the answers. I am allowed to feel uncertain and still take meaningful steps.

🕊️STAMP OF BRAVE BEGINNINGS

Stamp: Growth begins when courage outweighs comfort.

> ***Scripture:***
> *"By faith Abraham obeyed and went, even though he did not know where he was going."* – Hebrews 11:8

✨ RITUAL – The Boarding Pass Reflection

When facing a new beginning, reflect on the following:

> *What uncertainty am I facing right now?*
>
> *What skills or strengths have past experiences already given me?*
>
> *What small step can I take despite incomplete information?*

Write down one step you are willing to take and commit to acting on it.

🙏 PRAYER FOR TRUST IN TRANSITION

> *God, as I step into unfamiliar places, help me trust You beyond my understanding. Give me the courage to begin again, the humility to learn, and the perseverance to continue when growth feels uncomfortable. Guide my steps and shape my character through every transition. Amen.*

📓 REFLECTION CHECKPOINT

When have I been required to start over in an unfamiliar environment?

What fears surface when I lack clarity?

How has my past prepared me for my present transitions?

What does courage look like for me right now?

✨ LIFTED LESSON

Wisdom: You do not need certainty to lead—you need the courage to begin.

In Practice: Leadership growth accelerates when you move forward despite incomplete information.

Action: Identify one area of your life where hesitation has delayed progress and take one intentional step this week.

Scripture:
"Trust in the Lord with all your heart and lean not on your own understanding." – Proverbs 3:5

Chapter 5: Learning to Speak, Learning to Belong

Leadership Lesson: Communication is not about perfection or performance. Leadership begins when you listen well, speak with courage, and allow yourself to be seen before you are fully fluent.

Arriving Without a Voice

When I arrived in the United States, I spoke almost no English. I knew a few words—yes, no, thank you—but not enough to express who I was, what I had lived through, or what I hoped for. I had crossed continents only to find myself silent.

That silence was disorienting. I had always been observant and thoughtful, but now my inability to communicate made me feel invisible. In classrooms, conversations moved faster than my understanding. In social settings, I smiled politely while struggling to follow along. I felt present but not fully included.

For the first time, my intelligence and resilience were hidden behind a language barrier.

Being Placed Where Growth Was Unavoidable

I initially resisted staying in the United States. The challenge felt overwhelming, and returning to Rwanda seemed safer than starting over in a language I did not understand. My uncle listened patiently, then made a decision that changed everything.

He arranged for me to live with a host family who spoke only English.

There was no negotiation. No gradual transition. I was dropped into full immersion. I felt frustrated, exposed, and unprepared. Yet that discomfort became the catalyst for transformation.

The first evening, the family invited me to dinner and asked how my day had been. I could not answer. I sat quietly, overwhelmed by the effort it took to form even a simple sentence. Hours passed before I finally said, "I am sorry, but me tired."

They smiled, not with pity, but with encouragement. They told me that I had just spoken English—and that it was enough to begin.

Learning Through Humility and Persistence

Each day became an exercise in humility. Every evening, I wrote a short paragraph in French and translated it word by word using a dictionary. Before dinner, my host mother would help me correct it. Then I would read it aloud at the table.

The sentences were simple and imperfect. Yet each one represented progress.

I learned to listen carefully, not only to words but to tone, expressions, and body language. I learned to laugh at my mistakes instead of shrinking from them. I learned that fluency grows through effort, not avoidance.

Within weeks, silence gave way to sentences. Confidence followed gradually. I was still far from fluent, but I was no longer invisible.

Finding Belonging Through Courage

When I returned to my uncle's home, I was different. I could communicate enough to participate. I could ask questions. I could express basic thoughts. More importantly, I had learned that belonging is not granted through perfection—it is built through courage.

This experience reshaped how I understood leadership. I realized that communication is not about impressing others. It is about connecting with them. It requires vulnerability, patience, and willingness to be misunderstood along the way.

I also learned that effective leaders listen before they speak. They observe, adapt, and choose clarity over complexity. Language is not only about words; it is about presence and intent.

Faith and Identity in a New Language

Learning English was not just an academic challenge. It was an identity shift. Language shapes how you think, how you express emotion, and how you relate to others. As I learned new words, I learned new ways of seeing myself.

Faith remained central during this period. I prayed for patience, confidence, and courage. I asked God to help me trust the process rather than rush the outcome. Faith reminded me that growth often feels uncomfortable before it feels empowering.

This season taught me that leadership begins internally. Before influencing others, you must be willing to grow yourself. Before finding your voice publicly, you must first be willing to use it imperfectly.

What This Season Prepared Me For

Looking back, I see that learning to speak English prepared me for far more than academics. It prepared me for cross-cultural leadership, difficult conversations, and environments where clarity matters more than charisma.

It taught me how to enter rooms without certainty and still contribute meaningfully. It taught me that confidence grows from effort, not from ease. It also taught me to create space for others who are still finding their voice.

I did not know it then, but this season was shaping how I would later lead teams, mentor others, and navigate global environments.

The humility I learned through language would become one of my greatest leadership strengths.

🛂 VISA OF EXPRESSION – Permission to Be Heard Imperfectly

Visa Granted:
I give myself permission to speak even when my words are not perfect. My voice matters, and growth begins with participation.

🕊STAMP OF BELONGING

Stamp: Connection begins with courage, not fluency.

> ***Scripture:***
> *"Let your conversation be always full of grace."* –
> Colossians 4:6

✨ RITUAL – The Listening-First Practice

Before your next important conversation, pause and reflect:

> *Am I listening to understand or simply waiting to respond?*
>
> *What does this person need in order to feel heard?*
>
> *How can I speak with clarity rather than fear?*

Practice presence before performance.

🙏 PRAYER FOR COURAGE TO COMMUNICATE

God, thank You for the gift of communication in all its forms. Give me the courage to speak even when I feel unsure, and the humility to listen deeply. Help me use my voice to build understanding, create connection, and lead with grace. Amen.

📓 REFLECTION CHECKPOINT

When have I felt voiceless or misunderstood?

What fears do I associate with speaking up?

How can I become a more intentional listener?

Who helped me feel seen during a season of growth?

🌟 LIFTED LESSON

Wisdom: Leadership begins when you choose connection over perfection.

In Practice: Listening well creates trust faster than speaking confidently.

Action: In one conversation this week, focus entirely on listening before responding.

Scripture: *"Everyone should be quick to listen, slow to speak." – James 1:19*

Chapter 6: Dreams Rewritten in English

Leadership Lesson: Purpose outlives plans. Effective leaders hold vision with open hands and allow it to evolve without losing its meaning.

A Childhood Dream With Clear Shape

As a child growing up in Rwanda, I had a clear and specific dream. I wanted to become a news anchor. I imagined myself sitting behind a desk, speaking with confidence, delivering the news while the country listened. In our home, when the evening news came on, everything paused. The authority of the voice on the screen fascinated me. I wanted to be that voice.

That dream gave me direction. It shaped how I saw myself and how I imagined my future. It was not about fame as much as it was about impact. I wanted my voice to matter.

When I arrived in the United States, I carried that dream with me. Despite the language barrier, I enrolled at the University of Wisconsin–Platteville and declared journalism as my intended major. It felt like a continuation of what I had always believed about myself.

When Reality Interrupted the Plan

It did not take long for reality to challenge that vision. Journalism required more than interest or courage. It required fluency, nuance, and speed in a language I was still learning. I struggled to keep up with conversations, let alone imagine writing or broadcasting professionally.

The moment that shifted my thinking came unexpectedly. One evening, I was watching television with my uncle. When the news program appeared on the screen, I leaned forward, ready to engage. My uncle casually changed the channel. Then he changed it again.

I was surprised and asked why he did not want to watch the news.

He responded simply that there were many channels and that people chose what interested them.

That answer unsettled me. For the first time, I realized that having a platform did not guarantee influence. Even if I achieved my childhood dream, there was no assurance that people would listen.

My dream had been built on the assumption that attention was automatic. In this new context, I understood that impact required more than visibility.

Letting Go Without Losing Meaning

That realization forced me to ask difficult questions. If journalism was no longer the right path, what was? If my original plan no longer fit, what did purpose look like now?

My cousins suggested engineering. They saw my strength in mathematics and problem-solving and encouraged me to consider a field I had never imagined for myself. I did not fully understand what engineers did, but I trusted their perspective and was willing to explore.

Choosing engineering was not an emotional decision. It was a practical one. I needed a discipline that allowed me to grow professionally while continuing to develop my language skills. More importantly, I needed a direction that aligned with my evolving understanding of impact.

Signing up for engineering courses marked a significant shift. It required releasing a long-held identity and stepping into unfamiliar territory.

Discovering a Different Kind of Voice

Engineering challenged me in ways I had not anticipated. The coursework was demanding, the expectations were high, and the language barrier remained real. Yet something unexpected happened. I discovered that I enjoyed solving problems. I liked building systems and finding practical solutions.

I began to see that engineering offered a different kind of influence. It was not centered on being heard, but on making things work better. It was not about visibility, but about responsibility.

My voice did not disappear. It simply changed form. Instead of speaking through a microphone, I learned to communicate through designs, processes, and outcomes.

This shift reshaped my understanding of leadership. Influence does not require a spotlight. It requires contribution. Purpose does not always follow the path we imagine, but it remains present when we are willing to adapt.

Faith in the Pivot

Releasing my original dream was not easy. It required humility and trust. Faith played a quiet but critical role in that transition. I had to believe that letting go of one plan did not mean abandoning purpose altogether.

I learned that faith does not always confirm direction in advance. Sometimes it simply asks for obedience in motion. I trusted that God was still guiding my steps, even as the details changed.

This season taught me that leadership requires flexibility. Leaders who cling too tightly to their original plans risk missing the opportunities that align more closely with who they are becoming.

What the Pivot Prepared Me For

Looking back, I see clearly that this pivot laid the foundation for everything that followed. Engineering became the entry point into professional leadership, global work, and systems-level thinking. It gave me tools to solve problems and the credibility to lead in complex environments.

More importantly, it taught me to value impact over recognition. I learned that purpose is not tied to a single role or title. It is expressed through service, adaptability, and commitment to growth.

I did not abandon my dream. I allowed it to evolve.

I did not lose my voice. I learned how to use it differently.

I did not know it then, but rewriting my dream in a new language was preparing me for a future that required both humility and influence.

VISA OF EVOLUTION – Permission to Outgrow the Original Plan

Visa Granted:
I give myself permission to release plans that no longer fit and to trust growth that unfolds differently than expected.

🕊STAMP OF PURPOSE OVER PLAN

Stamp: Vision endures even when the path changes.

Scripture:
"In their hearts humans plan their course, but the Lord establishes their steps." – *Proverbs 16:9*

✨ RITUAL – The Dream Inventory

Set aside time to reflect on your current goals and aspirations:

Which dreams still align with who you are becoming?

Which plans may need to be released or reframed?

What new opportunities might be emerging as a result?

Write down one plan you are willing to loosen your grip on and one area you are willing to explore.

🙏 PRAYER FOR TRUST IN TRANSITION

God, thank You for guiding me through seasons of change. When my plans shift, help me trust that purpose remains. Give me the humility to release what no longer fits and the courage to follow where You are leading. Shape my vision beyond my expectations and align my steps with Your direction. Amen.

📓 REFLECTION CHECKPOINT

What dream have I had to release or redefine?

How did that shift create space for growth?

What does it mean to hold vision without rigidity?

Where might I be invited to trust a new direction?

✨ LIFTED LESSON

Wisdom: Purpose remains steady even when plans change.

In Practice: Flexibility allows leaders to respond to growth without losing direction.

Action: Identify one area where you are clinging to a plan and intentionally explore an alternative this week.

Scripture:
"See, I am doing a new thing." – Isaiah 43:19

Chapter 7: Blueprints and Breakthroughs

Leadership Lesson: Persistence is a leadership strategy. Competence is built through consistency, humility, and the willingness to keep going when progress feels slow.

Entering a Discipline I Did Not Yet Understand

When I officially committed to engineering, I did not fully understand what I was stepping into. I knew the coursework would be challenging and that the language barrier would continue to test me. What I did not yet grasp was how demanding the discipline would be—not only intellectually, but emotionally.

Engineering required precision, patience, and endurance. Lectures moved quickly. Technical terminology was unfamiliar. Group projects demanded collaboration in a language I was still mastering. There were days when I understood the concepts but struggled to follow the explanations, and days when I followed the words but not the logic behind them.

I often carried a French-English dictionary with me, translating textbooks line by line. Studying took twice the time and required twice the effort. Fatigue was constant. Doubt was frequent.

Yet, quitting was never an option.

When Persistence Became a Choice

There were moments when I questioned whether I belonged in that environment. I watched classmates grasp concepts more quickly and speak confidently in discussions. I felt behind, not because I lacked ability, but because the process demanded so much from me at once.

In those moments, I remembered what I had already survived. I remembered the refugee camps, the hunger, the uncertainty, and the nights when survival itself was in question. Compared to that, this challenge—however difficult—was one I could face.

Engineering school became a place where persistence was practiced daily. I learned that progress is rarely dramatic. It happens through repetition, discipline, and small victories that are easy to overlook.

Each concept mastered, each exam passed, and each lab completed reinforced a simple truth: endurance compounds over time.

Learning to Ask for Help

One of the most important lessons I learned during this season was how to ask for help. Early on, pride and fear made me hesitant. I did not want to appear incapable or slow. But isolation made the work harder, not easier.

Eventually, I began to approach professors during office hours. I joined study groups and asked classmates to explain concepts more than once. I learned to admit when I did not understand something rather than pretending that I did.

What I discovered was unexpected. Asking for help did not diminish my credibility. It strengthened it. Collaboration accelerated learning. Humility created connection.

This lesson would later become central to my leadership philosophy: strong leaders do not pretend to know everything. They build environments where learning is shared and support is mutual.

Seeing Engineering as Service

As my understanding grew, something shifted in how I viewed the discipline. Engineering was no longer just a collection of equations and assignments. It was a way of thinking about problems and designing solutions that improved how people lived and worked.

I began to see engineering as a form of service. Systems mattered because people depended on them. Precision mattered because safety and reliability were at stake. Excellence mattered not for recognition, but for responsibility.

This perspective transformed my motivation. I was

no longer studying simply to earn a degree. I was preparing myself to contribute meaningfully in environments where decisions carried real consequences.

Purpose began to replace pressure.

The Moment of Breakthrough

By the time I reached the later stages of my program, the work was still challenging, but it was no longer paralyzing. I understood the language of the discipline. I could participate in discussions, contribute to group work, and approach problems with confidence.

Walking across the stage to receive my engineering degree represented far more than academic achievement. It symbolized perseverance, adaptability, and faith carried through years of uncertainty.

I was celebrating every late night, every moment of frustration, every instance where I chose to stay instead of quit. I was honoring the version of myself who refused to be defined by limitation.

The breakthrough was not a single moment. It was the accumulation of countless decisions to continue.

What This Season Built in Me

Engineering did more than prepare me

professionally. It shaped how I approached complexity, pressure, and responsibility. It taught me how to break large problems into manageable parts and how to remain patient when solutions were not immediate.

It also taught me confidence rooted in competence rather than comparison. I learned that leadership credibility is built through preparation and consistency, not volume or visibility.

I did not know it then, but this season was laying the groundwork for leadership roles that required technical understanding, global collaboration, and resilience under pressure.

Blueprints and breakthroughs were never separate. One led to the other.

VISA OF PERSISTENCE — Permission to Keep Building

Visa Granted:
I give myself permission to continue building even when progress feels slow. I do not need perfection to move forward—only commitment.

STAMP OF BREAKTHROUGH

Stamp: Progress is built one decision at a time.

Scripture:
"Let us not grow weary in doing good, for at the proper time we will reap a harvest if we do not give up." – Galatians 6:9

✨ RITUAL — The Brick-by-Brick Reflection

At the end of each week, reflect on the following:

What challenge did I face this week?

What did I learn by staying engaged?

What small progress deserves acknowledgment?

Write these reflections down to track growth over time.

🙏 PRAYER FOR ENDURANCE AND GROWTH

God, thank You for the strength to persist through difficulty. When progress feels slow, remind me that growth is happening beneath the surface. Give me humility to ask for help, discipline to stay consistent, and faith to trust that my efforts are not wasted. Amen.

📓 REFLECTION CHECKPOINT

When have I been tempted to quit but chose to continue?

What role has persistence played in my growth?

How has asking for help strengthened my learning or leadership?

What am I building right now that requires patience?

✨ LIFTED LESSON

Wisdom: Persistence transforms effort into competence.

In Practice: Consistency builds credibility over time.

Action: Identify one area where steady effort will matter more than quick results and recommit to it this week.

Scripture:
"The testing of your faith produces perseverance." – James 1:3

Chapter 8: Paychecks and Purpose

Leadership Lesson: Excellence is a form of service. Meaningful work is not defined by status, but by responsibility, integrity, and impact.

Learning the Cost of Independence

One of the earliest lessons I learned in the United States was simple and sobering: independence comes with responsibility. Back home, my parents had carried the financial burden of my education and daily needs. In America, if I wanted to continue my studies, I had to work.

That reality arrived quickly. Tuition, housing, and basic expenses demanded action. I did not have the luxury of waiting for the perfect opportunity. I needed to contribute, immediately and consistently.

Work was no longer optional. It was part of survival—and part of growth.

Starting Where Opportunity Allowed

My first job was in the university cafeteria. I wore a hairnet and gloves, served meals to students who did not know my name, and cleaned tables long after the rush ended. The work was repetitive and physically demanding. It was also humbling.

Yet, that job represented something important. I was earning my own way. Every paycheck, no matter how small, represented dignity, responsibility, and progress.

Over time, I worked in the library and later as a math tutor. Each role brought new lessons. The library taught me consistency and quiet discipline. Tutoring revealed something unexpected: I enjoyed helping others understand concepts that had once challenged me.

Work became more than income. It became a place of learning and self-discovery.

Discovering Strength Through Service

Tutoring changed how I understood competence. I realized that mastery deepens when you help someone else learn. Explaining concepts required patience, clarity, and empathy. It required meeting people where they were rather than where I wished they were.

That experience reshaped my understanding of leadership. Leadership was not about being the smartest person in the room. It was about enabling others to grow.

I began to see that service and excellence were not separate ideas. Doing work well—regardless of visibility—was a way of honoring both responsibility and opportunity.

Entering the Professional World

After graduation, I entered the professional workforce as an engineer. Walking into that environment for the first time felt momentous. I had earned my place through years of discipline and persistence. Yet, I quickly realized that technical knowledge alone was not enough.

Professional work required collaboration, communication, and adaptability. Projects succeeded not only because of sound engineering, but because people trusted one another. Listening mattered as much as problem-solving. Humility mattered as much as confidence.

I learned to observe before acting and to ask questions before proposing solutions. These habits helped me build credibility and trust in environments where expectations were high.

Seeing Systems—and People—More Clearly

As I gained experience, I developed a strong interest in process improvement. I noticed inefficiencies and gaps and found myself asking why things were done a certain way. My goal was not disruption for its own sake, but improvement for the benefit of teams and outcomes.

This perspective required courage. Questioning established systems can be uncomfortable. It requires respect, timing, and clarity of intent. Over time, I learned how to frame ideas constructively and how to invite collaboration rather than resistance.

What emerged was a leadership approach grounded in service. I was not trying to impress. I was trying to make work easier, safer, and more effective for those involved.

Redefining Success

This season reshaped my definition of success. Titles and recognition became less important than contribution and integrity. I stopped measuring progress solely by advancement and started measuring it by impact.

Faith quietly informed this shift. I was reminded that work is not separate from purpose. Excellence is not about perfection or approval. It is about stewardship—using skills and opportunities responsibly.

A paycheck pays bills. Purpose sustains motivation. When the two align, work becomes meaningful rather than draining.

What This Season Clarified

Looking back, I see that these early work experiences grounded my leadership philosophy. They taught me humility, accountability, and respect for work at every level. They reinforced the belief that no task is insignificant when it serves a greater goal.

I did not know it then, but learning to work with integrity and intention would prepare me for larger responsibilities. Purpose did not arrive through promotion. It grew through consistency.

🛂 VISA OF SERVICE — Permission to Measure Success by Impact

Visa Granted:
I give myself permission to redefine success. I choose impact over approval and service over performance.

🕊️ STAMP OF PURPOSEFUL WORK

Stamp: Excellence is service in action.

> ***Scripture:***
> *"Whatever you do, work at it with all your heart, as working for the Lord."* — Colossians 3:23

✨ RITUAL — The Purpose Pulse Check

At the beginning of each week, reflect on:

> *What problem am I solving that truly matters?*
>
> *Who benefits from my work?*

How can I serve with greater intention this week?

Let these questions guide your focus and priorities.

🙏 PRAYER FOR MEANINGFUL WORK

God, thank You for the gift of work and the opportunity to serve through it. Help me approach each task with integrity and purpose. Remind me that excellence honors responsibility and that service creates lasting impact. Align my work with values that reflect humility, diligence, and care for others. Amen.

📓 REFLECTION CHECKPOINT

What was my first job, and what did it teach me about responsibility?

How has my understanding of success evolved over time?

Where am I called to serve with greater excellence?

How can my work reflect my values more clearly?

🌟 LIFTED LESSON

Wisdom: Meaningful work is rooted in service, not status.

In Practice: Excellence builds trust and creates impact over time.

Action: Identify one way you can improve a process, system, or experience for someone else this week and take the first step.

Scripture:
"Each of you should use whatever gift you have received to serve others." – 1 Peter 4:10

Chapter 9: The Power of Asking for Help

Leadership Lesson: Vulnerability is not weakness. Sustainable leadership is built through trust, delegation, and the courage to ask for support.

The Myth of Doing It Alone

For a long time, I believed that strength meant self-reliance. Survival had taught me how to endure, adapt, and carry responsibility without complaint. Asking for help felt unnecessary at best and risky at worst.

This belief did not come from arrogance. It came from experience. I had lived through seasons where support systems collapsed and survival depended on internal resolve. Independence became a form of protection.

However, what helped me survive was not always what would help me lead.

When Ambition Meets Capacity

Years into my professional career, I decided to pursue a master's degree in engineering program management. I wanted to grow as a leader and expand my ability to serve complex organizations. At the same time, I continued working full-time.

Initially, the challenge felt manageable. I was

motivated and energized by learning. Then my professional responsibilities increased. I was promoted into a role involving new component development within the engine division at John Deere. The work was demanding and often required international travel.

My schedule filled quickly. Weeks blurred together. Coursework, travel, and work competed for attention. Rest became optional. Progress slowed.

I reached a point where something had to change.

Recognizing the Breaking Point

One evening, after a long workday and travel schedule, I sat alone in a hotel room trying to complete an academic assignment. Exhaustion made focus nearly impossible. I considered postponing my degree and redirecting my energy entirely toward work.

Pausing would have been understandable. But something inside me resisted the idea of stepping away from growth simply because the season was difficult.

That moment forced an honest assessment. I could not sustain this pace alone. Continuing without adjustment would not demonstrate strength—it would guarantee burnout.

Choosing Vulnerability Over Pride

For the first time, I chose to ask for help deliberately.

I spoke openly with my manager about my workload and academic commitments. I communicated clearly with my study group and asked for flexibility when travel interfered with class schedules. I invited teammates to share responsibility rather than attempting to manage everything independently.

What happened surprised me.

Instead of questioning my capability, people responded with respect. Adjustments were made. Support emerged. Trust deepened.

Asking for help did not diminish my leadership. It strengthened it.

Redefining Strength in Leadership

This experience reshaped my understanding of leadership. Leadership is not about demonstrating endurance at the expense of sustainability. It is about creating systems where people can contribute effectively and support one another.

Delegation is not abdication. Vulnerability is not incompetence. Asking for help signals clarity, not weakness.

I learned that strong leaders model honesty about capacity. They create space for others to step up. They build trust through transparency rather than control.

Completing the Journey Together

With support in place, I completed my degree. Not because I worked harder than everyone else, but because I worked more wisely. I allowed others to participate in the process and shared responsibility where appropriate.

That season reinforced a truth I carry into every leadership role: progress accelerates when effort is shared.

I did not lose authority by asking for help. I gained partnership.

What This Season Taught Me

Looking back, I see that this chapter marked a shift from individual achievement to collective leadership. It taught me that long-term impact requires sustainable practices, honest communication, and mutual trust.

Survival taught me independence. Leadership taught me interdependence.

I did not know it then, but learning to ask for help would later shape how I lead teams, mentor others, and navigate complex systems.

🛂 VISA OF VULNERABILITY — Permission to Ask and Receive

Visa Granted:
I give myself permission to ask for help without shame. I am not required to carry everything alone.

🕊️ STAMP OF SHARED STRENGTH

Stamp: Leadership grows through shared effort.

> ***Scripture:***
> *"Two are better than one... If either of them falls down, one can help the other up."* — Ecclesiastes 4:9–10

✨ RITUAL — The Ask Inventory

Once a month, reflect on:

> *Where am I carrying too much alone?*
>
> *Who could I invite to share responsibility?*
>
> *What would it look like to delegate with trust?*

Write down one specific ask you will make this week and follow through.

🙏 PRAYER FOR HUMILITY AND WISDOM

God, thank You for placing people around me to support and strengthen me. Teach me to lead with humility rather than pride. Give me the courage to ask for help, the wisdom to delegate well, and the grace to receive support without guilt. Let my leadership reflect shared strength rather than silent struggle. Amen.

📔 REFLECTION CHECKPOINT

What beliefs have shaped my view of asking for help?

When has support strengthened my leadership?

How can I model vulnerability for those I lead?

Who in my life is ready to help if I give them permission?

🌟 LIFTED LESSON

Wisdom: Asking for help multiplies strength rather than diminishing it.

In Practice: Vulnerability builds trust and sustainability.

Action: Identify one area where you are overwhelmed and make a clear request for support this week.

Scripture:
"Carry each other's burdens." – Galatians 6:2

Chapter 10: The Woman Engineer in the Room

Leadership Lesson: Representation matters, but responsibility matters more. Leadership requires the courage to speak, the discipline to listen, and the integrity to create space for others.

Becoming Visible in Spaces Not Built for Me

As my career progressed, I began to notice something I could no longer ignore. In meetings, on project teams, and at professional events, I was often the only woman in the room. Sometimes, I was also the only person of color. I did not need to be told this; the absence of others like me made it obvious.

Visibility brought opportunity, but it also brought pressure. I felt an unspoken expectation to represent more than myself. My performance was sometimes interpreted as a reflection of others who were not present. That awareness shaped how carefully I prepared, how deliberately I spoke, and how thoughtfully I navigated professional spaces.

I learned quickly that presence alone was not enough. Leadership required intentional engagement.

Learning When—and How—to Speak

Early on, I observed more than I spoke. I wanted to understand the culture, the dynamics, and the unspoken rules of the room. I learned that timing mattered as much as content. Speaking up too quickly could be dismissed; waiting too long could result in missed opportunity.

When I did speak, I learned to be precise. I focused on clarity rather than volume. I grounded my contributions in data, preparation, and collaboration. Over time, credibility grew—not because I demanded it, but because I earned it consistently.

This season taught me an important leadership lesson: influence is built through trust, not force.

From Isolation to Advocacy

As I gained confidence, I began to notice others navigating similar challenges. Women entering technical roles. Early-career professionals unsure of their voice. Talented individuals hesitant to contribute because they felt out of place.

I recognized something familiar in them. Silence is rarely about lack of ability. More often, it reflects uncertainty about belonging.

Rather than accepting isolation as inevitable, I chose to act. I collaborated with others to create spaces where underrepresented voices could connect, learn, and support one another. These efforts were not about exclusion; they were about inclusion—ensuring that talent was recognized and developed equitably.

Leadership shifted from personal advancement to collective responsibility.

Carrying Identity Without Letting It Define Me

Being a woman engineer shaped my experience, but it did not define my capacity. I learned to hold my identity with confidence rather than defensiveness. I did not want to be known only for what made me different, but for the value I brought.

At the same time, I refused to minimize the importance of representation. Visibility matters—not for recognition, but for possibility. When people see someone like themselves leading, it expands what they believe is possible.

I did not know it then, but learning to lead in environments where I was underrepresented was preparing me for something broader. Navigating difference with humility, confidence, and awareness would later become essential beyond organizational boundaries.

Faith, Integrity, and Responsibility

Faith continued to shape how I led during this

season. It reminded me that leadership is not about proving worth, but about stewarding influence responsibly. I did not need to compete for space. I needed to contribute with integrity.

This perspective allowed me to lead without bitterness and advocate without resentment. I learned to challenge systems thoughtfully rather than react emotionally. Change required patience, credibility, and collaboration.

Leadership, I discovered, is not only about opening doors for yourself. It is about ensuring they remain open for others.

🛂VISA OF VISIBILITY – Permission to Lead Without Apology

Visa Granted:
I give myself permission to take up space with humility and confidence. I do not shrink to fit environments that need my contribution.

🕊️ STAMP OF RESPONSIBLE INFLUENCE

Stamp: Visibility creates responsibility.

> ***Scripture:***
> *"Let your light shine before others." – Matthew 5:16*

✨ RITUAL — The Seat-at-the-Table Reflection

Reflect on the following:

> *Where have I been invited to speak but hesitated?*
>
> *What perspective do I bring that others may not?*
>
> *How can I create space for voices that are often overlooked?*

Leadership grows when inclusion becomes intentional.

🙏 PRAYER FOR COURAGE AND WISDOM

> *God, thank You for entrusting me with influence. Give me courage to speak when it matters and wisdom to listen when others need space. Help me lead with integrity, humility, and responsibility. Let my presence create opportunity rather than pressure for those who follow. Amen.*

📓 REFLECTION CHECKPOINT

> *When have I felt the weight of representation?*
>
> *How have I responded to being different in professional spaces?*
>
> *Where am I being called to advocate rather than retreat?*
>
> *How can my leadership create access for others?*

✨ LIFTED LESSON

Wisdom: Leadership requires both visibility and responsibility.

In Practice: Influence grows when credibility and advocacy move together.

Action: Identify one way you can support or amplify another person's voice this week.

> ***Scripture:***
> *"Speak up for those who cannot speak for themselves." – Proverbs 31:8*

Chapter 11: Faith in the Workplace

Leadership Lesson: Values are most visible under pressure. Faith-informed leadership is not about visibility or persuasion, but about integrity, consistency, and trust.

Learning Where Faith Truly Shows Up

For much of my life, faith had been a personal anchor—something that grounded me privately during crisis, transition, and growth. As my professional responsibilities expanded, I began to realize that faith did not remain confined to quiet moments. It showed up in decisions, priorities, and how I treated people when outcomes were uncertain.

The workplace does not always welcome conversations about faith. In professional environments, belief can be misunderstood, minimized, or viewed as irrelevant. I learned quickly that faith did not need to be announced to be expressed. It needed to be embodied.

Leadership would test not what I believed, but how consistently I lived those beliefs.

Integrity When No One Is Watching

Early in my career, I noticed how easily small compromises were normalized. Cutting corners, shifting blame, or remaining silent when something felt wrong were often justified as pragmatism. These moments were rarely dramatic, but they were consequential.

I learned that leadership integrity is built in these small, quiet decisions. Faith shaped how I navigated them. It reminded me that short-term convenience can erode long-term trust, and that character is revealed when accountability feels costly.

I chose to speak honestly, even when it felt uncomfortable. I chose transparency over self-protection. I chose responsibility over recognition.

Those choices did not always lead to immediate reward, but they built credibility that lasted.

Leading Without Proselytizing

One of the most important lessons I learned was that faith-based leadership does not require persuasion. It requires consistency. People rarely need to know what you believe if they can see how you lead.

I focused on fairness, respect, and clarity. I treated colleagues with dignity, listened carefully, and honored commitments. I allowed my work ethic and decision-making to speak for themselves.

Over time, trust grew. Conversations deepened naturally. When questions arose about values, they emerged from relationship rather than agenda.

Faith was present, not imposed.

Ethical Tension and Courageous Clarity

There were moments when professional expectations conflicted with personal values. These situations required discernment rather than reaction. Faith did not provide easy answers, but it provided a framework for decision-making rooted in honesty, accountability, and respect for people.

I learned that ethical leadership does not always mean opposition. Sometimes it means asking better questions. Sometimes it means slowing down decisions to consider broader impact. Sometimes it means standing firm when compromise would undermine integrity.

In those moments, faith offered clarity, not certainty.

Creating Space for Others

As my leadership influence grew, I became more aware of my responsibility to create environments where others could bring their full selves to work. Not just their skills, but their values, perspectives, and experiences.

Faith informed this commitment. It reminded me that leadership is stewardship. Authority is entrusted, not owned. People perform best when they feel respected rather than managed.

I encouraged open dialogue, ethical reflection, and accountability without fear. This approach strengthened teams and built resilience, especially during periods of change.

Preparing for Leadership at Scale

I did not know it then, but these lessons were preparing me for leadership beyond familiar environments. Leading with integrity across cultures, systems, and expectations would require values that traveled well.

Faith anchored those values. It provided consistency in environments that varied widely. It reinforced humility, responsibility, and service—qualities that would become essential as leadership expanded beyond a single organization or country.

Before leadership could scale globally, it had to be grounded ethically.

🛂 VISA OF INTEGRITY — Permission to Lead With Conviction

Visa Granted:
I give myself permission to lead with integrity even when it requires courage. My values guide my decisions, regardless of external pressure.

🕊️ STAMP OF GROUNDED LEADERSHIP

Stamp: Integrity sustains influence.

> **Scripture:**
> *"The integrity of the upright guides them." – Proverbs 11:3*

✨ RITUAL – The Values Alignment Check

At the end of each month, reflect on:

> *Where did my actions align with my values?*
>
> *Where did I feel tension or compromise?*
>
> *What decision required courage rather than convenience?*

Write one intention for the month ahead that reinforces ethical clarity.

🙏 PRAYER FOR CONSISTENT LEADERSHIP

> *God, thank You for anchoring my leadership in values that endure. Give me wisdom to navigate complexity, courage to act with integrity, and humility to lead with service. Let my faith shape my decisions in ways that build trust and honor responsibility. Amen.*

📓 REFLECTION CHECKPOINT

How do my values show up in my daily work?

When have I faced ethical tension, and how did I respond?

What does integrity require of me in this season?

How can I lead in a way that creates space for others?

✨ LIFTED LESSON

Wisdom: Faith-informed leadership is expressed through integrity, not explanation.

In Practice: Consistent values build credibility across environments.

Action: Identify one value-driven decision you will make intentionally this week.

Scripture:
"Whoever walks in integrity walks securely." – Proverbs 10:9

Chapter 12: The Cost of Purpose

Leadership Lesson: Purpose carries a cost. Leadership matures when we acknowledge the weight of responsibility without resentment and choose faithfulness over comfort.

When Purpose Stops Feeling Light

Purpose is often described as energizing, clarifying, and fulfilling. Those descriptions are not wrong—but they are incomplete. Purpose also carries weight. Over time, that weight becomes noticeable, not because something is broken, but because responsibility has increased.

There came a season when I realized that living with purpose required more than commitment. It required endurance. The expectations were higher. The margin was thinner. The room for error felt smaller.

This was not a crisis. It was a reckoning.

Leadership narrows your circle.

As responsibility grows, fewer people can fully relate to the decisions you carry. You become careful about what you share and with whom. Not out of secrecy, but out of awareness. Some thoughts are not meant to be processed publicly.

There were moments when I felt alone—not because

I lacked community, but because leadership required discretion. I learned that loneliness is not always a sign of isolation. Sometimes it is the byproduct of stewardship.

Purpose asks you to carry things quietly.

Outgrowing Places and People

Purpose also creates distance.

Not everyone grows in the same direction or at the same pace. As my responsibilities evolved, some relationships naturally shifted. Conversations changed. Shared reference points faded.

This was not a failure of loyalty or love. It was a reality of growth.

Outgrowing familiar spaces can feel disorienting. There is grief in leaving what once fit comfortably. Purpose rarely announces these transitions ahead of time. It simply moves you forward, often before you feel ready.

Letting go was not rejection. It was obedience.

The Weight of Survival

Survival carries its own cost.

Having lived through loss, displacement, and rebuilding, I carried an awareness that never fully left me. Gratitude and grief coexisted. There were moments when I questioned why I had been given opportunities others never received.

Survivor's guilt is rarely loud. It surfaces quietly—in moments of success, recognition, or ease. Purpose intensifies this awareness. It asks difficult questions about responsibility and stewardship.

I learned that survival is not something to justify. It is something to honor by living well and serving faithfully.

Being Misunderstood

Purpose does not guarantee understanding.

There were seasons when decisions were questioned, motives misread, or silence interpreted incorrectly. Leadership invites scrutiny. Intent does not always translate clearly to others.

I learned that clarity does not ensure agreement. Being misunderstood is not a sign of misalignment; it is often the cost of leading thoughtfully rather than performatively.

Purpose requires the strength to remain grounded even when affirmation is absent.

Carrying the Role of "The Strong One"

Strength can become an expectation.

When you have navigated adversity, others often assume you will always be able to handle more. You become the dependable one. The composed one. The problem-solver.

There is honor in being trusted—but also exhaustion. Purpose requires discernment about when to be strong and when to ask for support. Carrying everything alone is not faithfulness; it is unsustainable.

I learned that strength must be stewarded, not displayed endlessly.

Faith Without Resolution

Faith does not remove the cost of purpose. It reframes it.

There were no moments where the weight disappeared entirely. What changed was my posture. Faith taught me to bring the weight into God's presence rather than carrying it alone.

Purpose is not meant to be painless. It is meant to be meaningful.

Faith does not promise comfort. It promises presence.

What the Cost Produces

Acknowledging the cost of purpose did not weaken

my commitment. It strengthened it. Naming the weight made it bearable. It allowed me to lead without resentment and serve without comparison.

Purpose refined my priorities. It taught me to rest intentionally, to choose wisely, and to measure success by faithfulness rather than approval.

The cost clarified what mattered most.

🛂 VISA OF HONESTY – Permission to Name the Weight

Visa Granted:
I give myself permission to acknowledge the cost of purpose without guilt or bitterness. Carrying responsibility does not require silence.

🕊 STAMP OF STEWARDSHIP

Stamp: Responsibility carried with humility builds endurance.

> ***Scripture:***
> *"Carry each other's burdens." – Galatians 6:2*

✨ RITUAL – The Cost Inventory

Set aside time to reflect on the following:

> *What responsibilities currently feel heavy?*

Where have I outgrown old patterns or spaces?

What support do I need to carry purpose well?

Write down one boundary you need to establish and one support you need to accept.

🙏 PRAYER FOR SUSTAINED FAITHFULNESS

God, thank You for entrusting me with responsibility. Help me carry it with humility rather than resentment. Give me wisdom to rest, courage to release what no longer fits, and faith to continue serving without losing myself. Let the cost of purpose refine me, not harden me. Amen.

📓 REFLECTION CHECKPOINT

What cost has purpose required of me?

Where have I experienced quiet loneliness in leadership?

What am I carrying that needs to be shared?

How can I steward strength without exhaustion?

✨ LIFTED LESSON

Wisdom: Purpose deepens through honesty, not denial.

In Practice: Acknowledging the cost prevents burnout and resentment.

Action: Identify one responsibility you need to carry differently this season and make a small adjustment this week.

Scripture:
"*My grace is sufficient for you.*" – 2 Corinthians 12:9

🔗Narrative Bridge to Chapter 13

The values I carried into the workplace would soon be tested beyond familiar systems and cultures. Leadership was about to expand beyond borders—and integrity would be its most essential guide.

Chapter 13: Leading Across Borders – Becoming a Global Leader

Leadership Lesson: Global leadership begins with humility. Influence across cultures requires listening before acting, understanding context before setting expectations, and respecting systems without losing accountability.

When Leadership Outgrew Geography

I did not set out to become a global leader. That title came later. What arrived first was responsibility that extended beyond one country, one culture, and one way of working.

As my role expanded, I found myself leading across borders—collaborating with teams whose languages, customs, and leadership norms differed from my own. At first, I assumed that good leadership principles translated universally. Clarity, accountability, and follow-through felt self-evident to me.

I soon learned that leadership at scale requires more than good intentions. It requires cultural intelligence.

The Day I Misread "Yes"

One experience during a business trip to China reshaped my understanding of global leadership.

I was in a meeting with a local team discussing an important action item. The timeline mattered. At the end of the discussion, I clearly stated that the action needed to be completed by the following day. Everyone in the room nodded and said "yes."

To me, that meant agreement and commitment.

Days passed, and the action remained incomplete. I felt frustrated and confused. From my perspective, expectations had been clearly communicated, and agreement had been expressed. What I interpreted as a lack of follow-through felt like a breakdown in accountability.

When I raised the issue with the local team, they responded politely—but firmly—with something I had not considered.

They explained that in their culture, hierarchy matters deeply. The main local leader had not been present in the room when I made the request. Because of that, no one else could commit to the task. Their "yes" had not meant agreement to complete the work. It meant acknowledgment that they had heard my request.

Commitment, they explained, must come from the senior local leader. Once that leader agrees, responsibility is assigned accordingly.

What I heard as a promise was, in fact, a courtesy.

The Moment of Realization

That conversation stopped me in my tracks.

The issue was not capability.
It was not resistance.
It was not lack of ownership.

It was my assumption that my leadership framework applied universally.

I had communicated clearly—but not contextually. I had expected alignment without fully understanding the system in which the team operated.

In that moment, I realized something critical: global leadership is not about exporting your leadership style. It is about learning how leadership already functions within a culture and working within that reality respectfully.

Adjusting Without Abdicating Responsibility

Learning this lesson did not mean lowering standards or avoiding accountability. It meant adjusting how leadership was exercised.

Going forward, I ensured that key local leaders were engaged early. I sought alignment at the appropriate level before setting expectations. I asked clarifying questions rather than assuming shared meaning.

Once commitment was established correctly, execution followed.

The work did not slow down. It improved.

Trust increased. Frustration decreased. Collaboration became more effective—not because expectations disappeared, but because they were communicated in a way that honored cultural structure.

What Global Leadership Requires

This experience taught me that global leadership demands three things:

> *First, **humility**. The willingness to admit that your way is not the only way—and sometimes not the right way in a given context.*
>
> *Second, **curiosity**. Asking questions before assigning meaning. Seeking understanding before expressing frustration.*
>
> *Third, **discipline**. Holding standards while adapting methods. Respecting systems without surrendering responsibility.*

Leadership across borders requires balance: flexibility without compromise, respect without passivity, authority without arrogance.

Carrying Values Across Cultures

Faith quietly guided me through this lesson. It reminded me that leadership is stewardship. Influence must be exercised with care, especially when it reaches beyond familiar environments.

Values such as respect, accountability, and integrity travel well—but how they are expressed must be adapted. Global leadership is not about abandoning who you are. It is about carrying who you are with greater awareness.

That experience in China reinforced something I had been learning all along: listening is not a leadership accessory. It is a leadership requirement.

What the World Has Taught Me

The world has taught me that leadership is contextual. What builds trust in one place may create tension in another. What feels direct in one culture may feel dismissive in another.

Effective global leaders do not assume universality. They practice awareness.

I did not lose credibility by learning this lesson. I gained it. Teams respond when they feel understood, respected, and led—not managed from afar.

🛂 VISA OF CULTURAL HUMILITY – Permission to Learn Before Leading

Visa Granted:
I give myself permission to pause, listen, and learn when leading across cultures. I do not need to have all the answers to lead well.

🕊 STAMP OF GLOBAL AWARENESS

Stamp: Understanding precedes influence.

> ***Scripture:***
> *"Let every person be quick to hear, slow to speak." – James 1:19*

✨ RITUAL – The Cultural Lens Check

Before setting expectations in a new environment, ask:

> *Who needs to be present for commitment to be real?*
>
> *How is authority exercised here?*
>
> *What does agreement actually mean in this context?*

Leadership improves when assumptions are examined.

🙏 PRAYER FOR WISE GLOBAL STEWARDSHIP

God, thank You for expanding my leadership beyond familiar borders. Teach me to lead with humility, wisdom, and respect. Help me listen deeply, learn continuously, and steward influence responsibly across cultures. Let my leadership reflect understanding before authority and service before control. Amen.

📓 REFLECTION CHECKPOINT

When have I assumed shared meaning that did not exist?

How do cultural systems shape leadership expectations?

Where do I need to listen more carefully before acting?

How can I lead with both clarity and humility in diverse environments?

🌟 LIFTED LESSON

Wisdom: Global leadership begins with understanding, not authority.

In Practice: Effective leaders adapt their methods without abandoning their values.

Action: Before your next cross-cultural interaction, seek clarity on how commitment and decision-making work in that context.

> ***Scripture:***
> *"From everyone who has been given much, much will be demanded."* – Luke 12:48

Chapter 14: Passport to Purpose

Leadership Lesson: Purpose is not a destination you reach; it is a responsibility you carry. Leadership begins when you understand that your journey is meant to serve others.

Understanding the Journey in Reverse

For much of my life, I thought purpose would reveal itself clearly and all at once. I imagined it arriving as certainty, clarity, or a title that made everything make sense. Instead, purpose unfolded slowly, through movement, disruption, and obedience.

Only in looking back did the pattern become clear.

Each chapter of my life—formation, survival, rebuilding, learning, leading—was preparing me for responsibility rather than recognition. Nothing was wasted. Every season contributed something essential.

Purpose, I learned, is rarely obvious while you are living it. It becomes visible in hindsight.

The Passport I Didn't Know I Was Carrying

A passport allows you to cross borders, but it does not tell you where to go or what to do when you arrive. It grants access, not instruction. Responsibility begins once the border is crossed.

My life had been shaped by borders—geographical, cultural, professional, and internal. Each crossing required adaptation. Each transition demanded humility. Each new environment revealed something about who I was becoming.

This book has traced those crossings. The passport was never the goal. The purpose was.

Leadership works the same way. Titles, roles, and opportunities grant access. Character determines impact.

Purpose as Stewardship

Over time, my understanding of purpose shifted. It stopped being about achievement and became about stewardship. What had been entrusted to me—education, opportunity, influence, survival itself—carried responsibility.

Leadership is not self-owned. It is borrowed. It must be exercised with care, integrity, and awareness of who is affected by its use.

This realization changed how I defined success. Advancement mattered less than alignment. Visibility mattered less than faithfulness. Purpose was no longer about what I accomplished, but about how I served.

The Role of Faith in the Long View

Faith remained the thread that held the journey together. Not as a constant sense of certainty, but as a consistent commitment to trust. Faith shaped how I navigated loss, transition, ambition, and responsibility.

It reminded me that leadership is not about control. It is about obedience in motion. It is about doing the next right thing with integrity, even when outcomes are unclear.

Faith did not remove struggle. It gave meaning to it.

What This Journey Offers the Reader

This book was not written to prescribe a single path. Your passport will not look like mine. Your borders, challenges, and callings will be different.

What remains universal is this:
Purpose grows where responsibility is embraced.
Leadership matures where humility is practiced.
Impact expands when service replaces self-focus.

You do not need to have everything figured out to move forward. You need clarity of values, willingness to learn, and courage to act.

Carrying Purpose Forward

If this journey has taught me anything, it is that leadership does not begin when you feel ready. It begins when you accept responsibility for the season you are in.

You may be in a season of formation, rebuilding, or transition. You may be carrying visibility, influence, or quiet responsibility. Wherever you are, purpose is present.

The question is not whether you have a passport. It is how you will use it.

🛂 VISA OF COMMISSIONING — Permission to Live With Intention

Visa Granted:
I give myself permission to live intentionally, to serve faithfully, and to lead responsibly wherever I am called.

🕊 STAMP OF PURPOSE

Stamp: Purpose is carried, not chased.

> ***Scripture:***
> *"Commit your work to the Lord, and your plans will be established." — Proverbs 16:3*

✨ RITUAL – The Purpose Inventory

Set aside time to reflect on the following:

What experiences have shaped my values?

What responsibilities have been entrusted to me?

Where am I being called to serve next?

Write one commitment that aligns your daily actions with your deeper purpose.

🙏 PRAYER OF SENDING

God, thank You for the journey that has shaped me and the purpose that continues to unfold. Help me steward what has been entrusted to me with humility and courage. Guide my steps across every border I encounter, and let my leadership reflect service, integrity, and faithfulness. Amen.

📔 FINAL REFLECTION

What season of the journey am I currently in?

What responsibility is mine to carry right now?

How can my leadership serve others more intentionally?

What does purpose look like in my daily life?

✨ LIFTED LESSON

Wisdom: Purpose is revealed through faithful stewardship over time.

In Practice: Leadership is exercised wherever responsibility is accepted.

Action: Take one intentional step this week that aligns your actions with your values.

> ***Scripture:***
> *"To whom much is given, much will be required." – Luke 12:48*

Chapter 15: The Prayer Before Every Journey

Leadership Lesson: Before movement comes alignment. Before leadership comes surrender. Prayer is not preparation for the journey—it is part of the journey.

A Pause Before Moving Forward

Every journey begins before the first step is taken.

It begins in stillness, in intention, and in awareness of what is being carried forward and what must be left behind. Over time, I learned that rushing into the next season without pausing to align my heart often led to unnecessary weight. Purpose requires movement, but wisdom requires pause.

This prayer became my way of pausing.

I return to it before travel, before decisions, before difficult conversations, and before transitions that carry uncertainty. It is not a prayer for certainty. It is a prayer for alignment.

The Prayer

God,

Before I go anywhere, I come to You.

Before I make plans, I pause.
Before I speak, I listen.
Before I act, I ask for clarity of heart.

I release the need to control outcomes.
I release the pressure to perform.
I release what no longer belongs to this season.

If I am carrying fear, steady me.
If I am carrying ambition, refine it.
If I am carrying responsibility, help me steward it well.

Go before me where I cannot see.
Stand beside me where decisions are heavy.
Remain behind me where I am tempted to return to what is familiar.

Teach me to recognize when it is time to move
and when it is time to wait.

Let my leadership be guided by humility,
my decisions shaped by integrity,
and my journey marked by service.

Where I am sent, let me arrive with respect.
Where I am welcomed, let me serve with gratitude.
Where I am challenged, let me respond with wisdom rather than fear.

If this journey is meant to stretch me, give me endurance.
If it is meant to refine me, give me humility.
If it is meant to bless others, keep me faithful.

I trust You with the path ahead,
even when the destination is unclear.

Amen.

Carrying the Prayer With You

This prayer does not belong to one moment.
It belongs to every beginning.

Return to it when:

- *clarity feels distant*
- *responsibility feels heavy*
- *leadership feels lonely*
- *transition feels uncomfortable*

Prayer does not remove uncertainty.
It grounds you within it.

🛂 VISA OF SURRENDER — Permission to Begin With Trust

Visa Granted:
I give myself permission to pause before moving

forward and to trust alignment over urgency.

🕊 STAMP OF STILLNESS

Stamp: Alignment precedes movement.

> **Scripture:**
> *"Trust in the Lord with all your heart and lean not on your own understanding." – Proverbs 3:5*

✨ PRACTICE – The Pre-Journey Pause

Before your next transition, decision, or difficult conversation:

1. *Stop for one full minute.*
2. *Read this prayer slowly.*
3. *Ask yourself: What am I carrying that needs to be released?*

Begin only after you have paused.

🌟 LIFTED LESSON

Wisdom: Prayer is not an escape from leadership; it is a grounding for it.

In Practice: Leaders who pause before moving forward lead with greater clarity and care.

Action: Use this prayer before your next journey—physical, professional, or internal.

Chapter 16: Home Is Not a Place

Leadership Lesson: Belonging is not tied to geography. Home is formed through alignment, purpose, and the courage to carry identity across change.

Searching for What Could Not Be Rebuilt

For a long time, I believed home was something that could be returned to. A place you left, rebuilt, or reclaimed. I imagined that one day I would arrive somewhere and feel fully settled again—rooted in a way that erased the memory of movement.

That belief made sense. My life had been shaped by displacement, transition, and crossing borders. Wanting a place that felt permanent was not a weakness. It was a longing.

But over time, I learned that the version of home I was searching for no longer existed—not because it was taken from me, but because I had changed.

When Belonging Becomes Internal

Each transition taught me something important. Home was not restored through geography. It was restored through identity.

I began to notice that I could feel grounded in unfamiliar places when my values were clear. I could feel unsettled in familiar spaces when alignment was missing. Belonging was not about comfort. It was about coherence—living in a way that matched who I had become.

Home, I realized, was not a destination. It was a state of alignment.

Carrying Home Forward

As my life expanded across cultures, roles, and responsibilities, I stopped asking where I belonged and began asking how I was living. When my actions reflected integrity, service, and faith, I felt at home—even in places that were new.

This shift changed how I approached leadership. I no longer led from a need to prove or secure belonging. I led from groundedness. From purpose. From an internal sense of home that did not depend on external validation.

Leadership became less about arrival and more about presence.

Identity Without Attachment

Letting go of a fixed idea of home did not mean losing my roots. It meant carrying them differently. My history, culture, and experiences did not disappear as I moved forward. They traveled with me, informing how I listened, how I led, and how I connected.

I learned that identity does not need a permanent address. It needs integrity.

Home became something I brought with me—into meetings, communities, decisions, and relationships. It lived in how I treated others and how I honored where I came from without being bound to where I had been.

Peace Without Permanence

There is peace in accepting that some lives are shaped by movement. Not everyone is meant to stay in one place, role, or version of themselves. Some callings require flexibility, openness, and the willingness to belong without settling permanently.

This realization did not create restlessness. It created freedom.

When home is internal, movement no longer threatens identity. Change becomes a companion rather than a disruption.

What Home Means Now

Home is where my values are lived.
Home is where my faith is practiced.
Home is where responsibility is carried with humility.

Home is not a place I return to.
It is a posture I live from.

🛂 VISA OF BELONGING — Permission to Be Grounded Wherever You Are

Visa Granted:
I give myself permission to belong without permanence and to carry home within me.

🕊 STAMP OF ROOTED IDENTITY

Stamp: Home is carried, not found.

> **Scripture:**
> *"The Lord will watch over your coming and going."* – Psalm 121:8

✨ PRACTICE — The Belonging Check

When you feel unsettled, ask yourself:

> *Am I seeking comfort or alignment?*
>
> *What value anchors me right now?*
>
> *How can I live from who I am, not where I am?*

Grounding begins internally.

🙏 PRAYER FOR ROOTEDNESS

> *God, thank You for walking with me through every place and season. Teach me to carry home within me—to live from alignment rather than attachment.*

Wherever I go, let my presence reflect peace, integrity, and purpose. Help me belong deeply, even in moments of change. Amen.

✨ LIFTED LESSON

Wisdom: Belonging is built through alignment, not location.

In Practice: Leaders grounded in identity remain steady through change.

Action: Identify one value that anchors you regardless of where you are and live from it intentionally this week.

Chapter 17: The Journey Continues

Epilogue

There is no final arrival point to a life lived with purpose.

Journeys evolve. Responsibilities shift. Seasons change. What once required courage may one day require patience. What once demanded rebuilding may later call for stewardship. Purpose does not end—it adapts.

This book closes here, but the journey it describes does not.

You may have read these pages looking for clarity, confirmation, or courage. Perhaps you recognized parts of your own story in mine. Perhaps you are standing at a border—geographical, professional, relational, or internal—wondering what comes next.

If there is one truth I hope remains with you, it is this:

You do not need the entire path to take the next faithful step.

Purpose rarely announces itself in full.
It unfolds through responsibility accepted, values lived, and service offered—often quietly, often imperfectly.

Leadership is not reserved for moments of visibility.
It is practiced in consistency, integrity, and humility—especially when no one is watching.

You will cross borders you did not anticipate.
You will outgrow versions of yourself you once relied on.
You will carry weight you did not choose but were entrusted with.

None of this means you are off course.

If the journey asks more of you than you expected, pause.
If the path feels unclear, listen.
If the responsibility feels heavy, share it.

You are allowed to move forward without certainty.
You are allowed to rest without guilt.
You are allowed to grow beyond what once defined you.

Purpose is not something you complete.
It is something you live.

And so the journey continues—not away from who you are, but deeper into it.

Go forward with humility.
Lead with integrity.
Serve with faithfulness.

Carry home within you.
Carry purpose with intention.

And when the road changes—as it will—pause, realign, and keep going.

●●●

FINAL STAMP

The journey continues.

About the Author

Clémentine Uwineza is a global leader, engineer, and faith-driven mentor. A survivor of genocide and former refugee, she rebuilt her life in the United States through education, perseverance, and faith.

Her career spans heavy manufacturing and the aerospace and defense industry, and her work has taken her to more than forty countries across nearly every continent. Known for leading with compassion and global perspective, she is passionate about developing leaders who uplift others.

In 2025, Clémentine experienced a transformative baptism in the Holy Spirit that deepened her calling to serve, empower, and lead with purpose.

www.ingramcontent.com/pod-product-compliance
Lightning Source LLC
La Vergne TN
LVHW090529110826
845146LV00003B/1037